A Bouquet of Love
Essence of Sweet Heart & Mind

S Afrose

Ukiyoto Publishing

All global publishing rights are held by

Ukiyoto Publishing

Published in 2024

Content Copyright © S Afrose

ISBN 9789360497118
*All rights reserved.
No part of this publication may be reproduced,
transmitted, or stored in a retrieval system, in any form
by any means, electronic, mechanical, photocopying,
recording or otherwise, without the prior permission of
the publisher.*

The moral rights of the authors have been asserted.

*This is a work of fiction. Names, characters, businesses,
places, events, locales, and incidents are either the
products of the author's imagination or used in a fictitious
manner. Any resemblance to actual persons, living or
dead, or actual events is purely coincidental.*

*This book is sold subject to the condition that it shall not by
way of trade or otherwise, be lent, resold, hired out or
otherwise circulated, without the publisher's prior
consent, in any form of binding or cover other than that in
which it is published.*

www.ukiyoto.com

To my Dear Readers
Planet of Words

"Take my love.
Lead a beautiful life
With your dear heart.
Happy Valentine!"

Acknowledgement

Thanks a lot Dear Almighty for blessing me always.

Thank you so much dear parents, friends, readers, well wishers.

Without any drop of the divine love, I can't be able to walk smoothy onward.

Take the purest essence of my love.

© S Afrose

Dhaka, Bangladesh, 24th Jan'24.

"Fragrance Of Words"

Nothing is dear,
When life cries
For the essence of love.
Everyday fills
With beautiful thoughts.
A bouquet of flowers
Turns into
A bouquet of love.
Just be its owner,
Let's spread
Essence of sweet heart & mind.

A Bouquet of Love... *a poetry book, spreads the sweet fragrance of love as the eternal shower.*

For example- A Bouquet of Love, Be the Rose, Luminous etc.

Love is the crucial fact for the dearest life, at each aspect of the dreamy site.

Hope, anyone will love it for a second, if tries to spend some beautiful moments.

 (For any kind of unexpected words, just forgive)

Thanks!

From Author Desk ♥

© S Afrose, BD. 24th an'24.

Contents

A Bouquet of Love	1
Bouquet Of Roses	4
Be The Rose	6
Black Rose	8
Take My Love	10
The Mystic Gift Box	11
Icon Of Love	13
Luminous	14
Lost The Love	15
Togetherness	17
Valentine	18
Love, A Drop Of Love.	20
So Special	23
Weather Of Love	25
How Much!	28
Aurora	30
Will You Accept?	32
In My Hands	34
Saw	36
Those Bluish Eyes	39

Just Feel It	41
Four Eyes	43
Without The Border	45
Yellow to Green	47
Red Vase	49
Value Your Tears	51
A Glimpse Of Your Smile	53
Love You	55
The News Of Heart	57
I Can't Live	59
May Be	60
Opinion	61
Open The Door	63
A Blue Feather	65
Really Picky	67
No One	69
Lost Love	71
Really	73
Kindly Check The Box	75
Write From Heart	76
About the Author	*79*

A Bouquet of Love

The allegation is not right
That sight is not for the fight.
A new look, A new drape,
Take this moment as a new trend.

A bouquet of love
It's all over the previous verses.
Lost smile once a time,
Now see the desired sunshine.

Happy look, Happy news,
Happy Valentine! Oh sweetheart!
A bouquet of love!
For you all, For the dearest hut.

What's that hut?

Who will be there?
Anyone, with sweet thoughts.
Anyone, with beautiful heart.

Heart! Oh dear!
You can't escape for this time,
The fume of the love,
Covers the azure's canvas.

The galactic canvas,
Holds all at a time,
No sanctions for any part,
When love is the fragrance of sweet life.

A bouquet of love!
A castle of heart!
A slope of dreams!
Imagine! Seen.

May be this time,

Best for the rest.
To be happy always,
Holding the sweet essence.

A bouquet of love!
Come on dear universe.
See and capture this caption,
This is crucial for each junction.

Without love nothing can exist,
May be tormented, all along the life's road.
Need to accept this term,
Love can conquer any unwanted sign.

Open the closed door of heart,
Make the cosmic ray of love,
People will never leave this part,
Love is the core point with respect and trust.

(4th Jan'24)

Bouquet Of Roses

Take this bow
A new paw
Views of life.

Voucher of life
Blank or not
BOUQUET of roses.

A free moment
A friend
A little triumph.

A fresh start is essential
As the switch board of life
Once lost.

Then...

Below the dove
Your edited version
Desired hub.

BOUQUET of roses
For this time
Keep up dear mind.

(1ˢᵗ Jan'24)

Be The Rose

Forward
The desired bridge,
Trying
To pass,
But...

Something happens.
Can't move on.
A shackle
Trying,
To hold on.

Be the rose.
Rising emotions,
Spreading thoughts.
Risk factors, as usual?
No matter.

Be the rose.
Use each thorn
For the protection,
Any caption,
For the new sunshine.

(1st Jan'24)

Black Rose

Rare.
Of course,
As you know
You can do that.
Mentioned Once.

The black rose is here
Dear
Hear
Gear up...far.

Back to back
A new feedback,
You get that
Without any prospective state.

The black rose is fine.
The black rose is rare treasure.
That treasure is inside your mind.

Rare
And so precious.

(1st Jan'24)

Take My Love

Hello dear
My sweet mind,
Take this flower
Take my love.

I know
You are rare,
So beautiful
So precious.

Take this bow
My dear heart,
Love you dear
Take my love.

(1st Jan'24)

The Mystic Gift Box

A box
So red,
Decorated by red roses
Full of mystery.

The myth of love!
Happy Valentine!

Dedicated to dear all,
No more collisions.
A better equation
For this time.

Take care
The box,
Pick your
Desired essence of heart.

(1ˢᵗ Jan'24)

Icon Of Love

This red rose
Amidst the frost zone,
Acts as a miracle,
To show all,
Love can exist anywhere,
As a perpetual ride.

Icon of love
The red heart.
The red vibe
The red rose,
My dear.

(1ˢᵗ Jan'24)

Luminous

Luminous this time!
The person
The moment.

You are in my heart
You are mine,
Your love is eternal
You are my earth.

Luminous this time!
Your each word,
Your eyes,
Your existence on the earth.

(1st Jan'24)

Lost The Love

The frozen moment.
Heart craving
Only for you,
As you're
My oxygen.
To be here
Always.

Suddenly,
The lost channel.
The lost mind
The lost heart,
Lost the love.

Ah!
So painful.
So unfathomable.

How can accept?
Lost the happiness,
Lost the love.

(1st Jan'24)

Togetherness

Together,
They can make
The paradise;
Within any site.

The essence of love!

Togetherness
With hope and trust,
They can play any role
With smile.

The magic of love!

 (1st Jan'24)

Valentine

Dear!
Hold my hands.
Feel my love.
My heart beats so fast,
Wants to cuddle you.
That moron face!
Not acceptable,
My valentine!
You're my valentine!

Say something.
See, love sparks all over.
Right?
For me every day is such a special one.
Can you halt the Ocean?
Love is the uncontrolled ocean of sweet life.
My love!

Universal from pristine to onward.
Try to understand my feelings.
Without you, my candle will extinguish.
My life would be hopeless,
My existence must be vanished.

My heart can't beat anymore.
Only a broken mirror to reflect agony!

(4th Jan'24)

Love, A Drop Of Love.

Today for you and I
Not for all the time,
Need to remind this part
Today is very special.

Not for this moment,
A moment is so special.
Happiness or Love,
Today is your turn.

Happy day,
Happy ray,
Happy bay,
This moment is perpetual.

A chance.
Always?

Today is perfectly smile,
Better to best.

Give it a try,
You don't know, why?
Today is valentine.
Part of the historic rhyme.

What's the valentine?
Want to see a clear picture.
Love for a particular day?
It's not right.

Live with love,
A drop of love is enough,
To show the magic,
Holding all by the same knot.

That's the love, a drop of love.
For everything for everyone

For every moment in this life,
That's the love.

(4th Jan'24)

So Special

Dear!
You cover my entire world,
With the essence of angelic flowers.
So special.

A cosy moment
Your favourite scent,
The petals of rose.
So special.

A tremendous flow
In the heart,
Your sparkling existence
So special.

Every day is special
When you smile,

With vivid layers
Thoughts of mind.

Nothing is here
Except the silly heart,
The blooming rose
Meadow of life.

Shimmering beauty!
Promise,
Exceptional mirth,
At each birth in the planet.

The string of love,
As the guitar plays in my heart,
And we enjoy the rhythms,
Mind touches the cosmic ride.

(4th Jan'24)

Weather Of Love

Silly caption
Hold on
Change that perception.

Melody of life is here
Lying
And Calling…

The day is over
Sun says goodbye dear heart.

Darkness covers.
Amidst all
A lonely soul.
A lengthy sigh!

Ah!
Ah!
Ah!

From where, can find true love?
From where?
Where????

Mutual trust & respect,
Without any surreptitious thought.
May touch my heart.
Still waiting for that golden moment.

Sea shorelines!
Hope, any mystic call.
The sun welcomes again
With new ray,
With new verse.

Don't regret.

Change that perception.
A bit more,
Endurance!
For this verse.

Ahead,
The favourite lane.
The piano of mind
Once lost,
Now it is found here.

The sign of life
The sign of love,
Don't mix up
Annoying vibes,
As this is the weather of love.

(4th Jan'24)

How Much!

Hold my heart
Let us fly
A spark.

A new verse
Exceptional waver
A soulful promise.

Be my valentine
Heart speaks
Amorous love!

Let me give a hug
Let me take a sweet ride
Let me spread my heart.

Let me tell the dreamy cascade
Let me fly as butterfly
Let me tell you, how much I love!

(4th Jan'24)

Aurora

The night sky.
Fragrance of darkness.
Aurora...unbelievable
Unless locked,
My soul.

In my heart
Thought,
There must be
A fallen dream.
Wow!

Luminous time.
Mystic happiness,
Myriad hues.
In my mind
A painting is ongoing.

Soliloquy!
Oh!
How beautiful!
Aurora
The night vibe.

(4th Jan'23)

Will You Accept?

Just a mere question
Will you accept
This time?
My rhyme
Just a little gift,
A bare rose
Or a garland of bakuls.

Will you accept?
As my apology
For the fresh part
Of this art.
Pls don't make a noise,
This will destroy
The beautiful ride of the doves.

Will you come?
Will you see?
Will you able?
Will you???

(4ᵗʰ Jan'24)

In My Hands

Crazy I am.
Crafted
The little gem.
In my hand,
Ouch!

Bleeded my hands,
Still can't stop
To hold this challenge.
For proving
This is most important time.

Make this day
Your favourite say,
Then can be there

With your layer.
Just look at here, in my hands.

(4ᵗʰ Jan'24)

Saw

That was rare.
Shooting stars
Fallen flowers.
Starry night
With heavenly shower.

Saw
Raw,
Paw
Claw.
Then Bow...

Actually
Myself,
Not
Yourself.
So?

Saw
Surprised.
Booked
Dear mind
For whom?

Don't be shocked.
Disappointed!
If there's
Only the barren zone.
Oh no!

Saw
And thought,
Gradually
Accept

Then can feel-
Just wow!!!

(4th Jan'24)

Those Bluish Eyes

Never seen these arts
Those bluish eyes.

Is that the ocean,
Full of myths of life?

No!
This is the regular part of life.

How comes?
Newcomer?

Those bluish eyes
Your favourite guide.

Help to see
Dreams and colourful flies.

Eyes?
Really?

Just wow!
Sweet passion.

Those bluish eyes
The favourite riders.

(4th Jan'24)

Just Feel It

I have no idea
What's going on?
Midst the river
A new boat.

No rider
No one there,
To hold
The sail.

Just feel it.
See the point,
What's that?
Just feel it.

I know I can,
You know you can,
But for some moments;

The lost essence.

Just feel it
And believe.
Below the sky
The bay of life.

(24th Jan'24)

Four Eyes

There are two eyes
For you
For me.

There are four eyes
For you,
Not for me.

I see.
At a glance
I can help,
I can understand.

Obviously you are right,
Not all the time.
The tube is empty,
The mind is blank.

No
Never.
Don't say like this part,
There are so adorable arts.

There are four eyes.
You see,
I see;
The desired bridge of mind.

(24th Jan'24)

Without The Border

Without the border
I see,
Something is so fissy;
Mystic part.

I can see
Nobody is near.

Without the border
Who can help?
Who will help?

Hello!
Anyway,
No answer.

Help me!
I will do.

Oh God!

Bless me!
Don't be shocked.
I will be here.

Without the border
You know,
I know.

It will be alright.

(24th Jan'24)

Yellow to Green

When mind cries,
Each dream turns
Green to Yellow sight.

When dream smiles,
Each one turns
Into the rhythms of mind.

Yellow to Green
Or
Green to Yellow,
What do you like?

Of course
I like,

That's the sweet pie.
Greenish petals.

(24th Jan'24)

Red Vase

Once a sweet shade
Shaking the pocket,
So many dirty arts,
Must clean sweetheart;
Forever.

Red vase on that corner,
Waiting for the sweet flowers
For the dearest love.
A new beginning
Of course.

Heart says
Hi,
Love me as usual.

I am the holder
Of the sweet lovely life.

(24th Jan'24)

Value Your Tears

Shedding tears?
Why?
I will not allow this time.
I will not tolerate anymore.
The gusty touch!

Do you sure about that?
Get it.
Then relax.
Whatever,
You will know that at last.

The beautiful moment,
The beautiful time.
Love this part

With dearest heart,
Value your tears.

(24th Jan'24)

A Glimpse Of Your Smile

Just believe this time,
It will be
Your favourite rhyme.
Yes.

A glimpse
Of your smile,
Just wow!
Making the crescent verse.

Just believe your mind.
You know
It's fine,
When you smile.

Am I wrong?
No.

Then,
Sorry for my words.

A glimpse!
A glimpse of your smile,
Enough,
For making the good vibes.

(24th Jan'24)

Love You

How many times?
How much?
You will see,
You have to realize.

Love you!
Love you!

You are my whole earth.
My base of the paradise.
My eternal happiness!

Back to back
On the stage,
I cried once
For a long.

No one comes
To wipe
My tears,
I received my love.

Hello dear!
Don't cry,
I love you.
Yes, love you so much.

(24th Jan'24)

The News Of Heart

When sun says
It's time,
Good morning.
I say,
Where is my sunshine?
It smiles.
I know
You called your love.

He is here
Or She is here.

Who is he or she?
The messenger
For your smile,
For starting the day of life.
Wow!

Really amazing,
The news of heart.

(24th Jan'24)

I Can't Live

Yes that is fine
When heart says,
I will not be here
Without you.

I can't live
Pls accept the fact.

You are no more
How can conclude
My dream?
My earth?

I can't live
I can't.

(24th Jan'24)

May Be

May be this time-
I will be fine
I have signed.

Got it,
Also felt it.
I have signed.

It's fine.
Never mind
I thought.

Got it
Never mould this thing.
Sought it.

(24th Jan'24)

Opinion

Your opinion
Is the most prominent,
Never lose'
When you get
The potion.

Your opinion,
Never lose the hope.
When you see
And guess,
What's your opinion?

I know.
I knew.

I have attached
From the so past,
Now you see that dear.

(24th Jan'24)

Open The Door

The vast sky!
From so far can see and hear.
Congrats sweetheart,
In the deepest mind,
Open the door of heart.

Yes!
Open the door of heart.
Open the door of mind.
Feeling and sealing,
Literally a thing,
Open the door of mind.

Open the door of earth,
Open the door of heart,
Open the door of love,

Open the door of sweet mart.
So, find out the best of your heart.

(24th Jan'24)

A Blue Feather

Don't go away as usual.
Don't make the noise.
Don't make this time.
A strong rhyme,
A strange feeling.

A blue feather!
A blue treasure!
Jig jag thoughts,
A blurred phase.

Make it clear
A blue frame,
A blue picture,
A blue feather.

Love & love,
Glittered pearls.

Wings of dream
Wings of mind.

(24th Jan'24)

Really Picky

Hahahaha!
Really picky
When you see.
When you saw,
Really picky.
Really?

I wish
For the best,
I wish
For the rest.
As per your time,
As per your sight.

I hope
Journey of joy,
Mirror of mind,
Reflection of the sunshine.

Really picky
Really stingy,
Really wish
Really sorry.

(24th Jan'24)

No One

Share and care
No one is here.

Share and care
I will be here.

Share and care
Who is here?
Share and care
I will not be here.

Idea!
Once I was attached,
Now can't.
I have lost.

Share your experiences.

Share your love.
Share your heart,
Share your pain.

Share your dream
Share your love,
Share your part
Share your feelings.

(24th Jan'24)

Lost Love

When the moon smiles
I cry.
Asking,
My lost love?
Where?
Give me back,
Come back in my life.

When the moon smiles
I say,
I will not be here;
If can't get
The lost love.

Lost love!
My sweet chime.
Need to help

Need to share,
The world of mine.

(24th Jan'24)

Really

O'
I see.
It's your
And realize,
Really it's you.

O'
I see.
I saw
I told,
It's me.
Really it's me.

Believe this
Access this
Accept this.
Love this.

O'
I see
It's you.
Really it's you.

(24ᵗʰ Jan'24)

Kindly Check The Box

A letter
Send
Into your account
Of the heart.
The mail box.
Kindly check the box.

Yes try,
Yes true.
Love this fact.
Kindly check the box.
Kindly check the process of mind,
Kindly check the process of heart.
Finally it would be set.

(24th Jan'24)

Write From Heart

It's a great art.
The part of life
The part of love.

Write from heart.
Make it
Love it.

Write from heart.
You know that
I know that.

Write from heart.
Love each part
Love your thoughts of sweet life.

Love your words.
Writing room!
Write from heart.

(24th Jan'24)

About the Author

S Afrose

Author S Afrose (Sabiha Afrose, from Bangladesh) has made her writing realm since August-2020.

She enjoys each of the part of this writing ward. She tries to express the hidden word or emotion, by her words; with the glamour of poetry. Poetry is her best friend.   Her writes have been publishing on magazines and anthologies (90+). In this writing realm, she has achieved many awards (beyond her expectations eg. Doctorate in Literature from

Instituto Cultural Colombiano, Literoma Laureate Winner 2022, Mahatma Gandhi Award 2023 from Instituto Cultural Colombiano, One of the World Record Holders for Hyperpoem, etc.)

Published author of poetry books- **Thanks Dear God, Poetic Essence, Reflection of Mind, Glittering Hopes, Angels Smile, Tiny Garden of Words, Dancing Alphabet, Artistic Muse, Essence of love, The Magical Quill, Dear Children, Haunted Site. Woman, The Butterfly, A Little Fantasy, Lion's Roar, The Bride, No War, Lost Lotus, Friendship, Happy Christmas, A New Beginning, Bluish Ocean, Stop Discrimination.**

All are available worldwide (on Amazon.com & from publication hub and from other sites-Flipkart, Bookshop, Booksgoogle, Barnesandnobles etc. also, as any format). Apart these, there are some Bengali and English poetry books (available on rokomari.com in Bangladesh).

Her mother is Selina Begum and father is Manirul Islam.

Educational achievements- B Pharm, M Pharm from Jahangirnagar University, Bangladesh.

Hobbies are reading, writing, specially the paradise of the poetic flowers.

Contact-afrosewritings@outlook.com,
sabiha_pharma@yahoo.com

You Tube: S Afrose *Muse of Writes*(@safrose_poetic_arts)

Facebook page: Muse of Words by S Afrose

Twitter:@afrose2020

Inst. @safrosepoetryworld

**"THANK YOU SO MUCH
FOR BEING MY DEAR FRIEND"
MY LOVE!
MY POETRY PARADISE!**

www.ingramcontent.com/pod-product-compliance
Lightning Source LLC
LaVergne TN
LVHW041537070526
838199LV00046B/1710